ORPHA

ALSO BY JULIAN TURNER

Crossing the Outskirts

(2002)

Julian Turner
Orphan Sites

ANVIL PRESS POETRY

Published in 2006
by Anvil Press Poetry Ltd
Neptune House 70 Royal Hill London SE10 8RF
www.anvilpresspoetry.com

This book is published with financial assistance
from Arts Council England

Designed and set in Monotype Dante by Anvil
Printed in Great Britain at
Alden Press Ltd, Oxford and Northampton

ISBN 0 85646 384 1

BLESSING

for Bryony

Daughter I wish you words as rich as this:
a smorgasbord of sense, it both connotes
a bare-boned pleasure and the hint of *haute
cuisine*, all taste condensed into a kiss.

Just as money is the root of evil,
it is the root of money, its clear matrix
the union of two radical things. A small
amount denotes a recipe for sceptics;

a good luck charm; vivacity like lemon;
a quality of spirit manifest.
Used in holy water's preparation,
sin-eaters placed it on a corpse's chest

to sieve his sin before they buried him.
It will glow white within the darkest pit.
Odysseus sowed it as a strategem.
It has the taste of tears. I wish you it.

ACKNOWLEDGEMENTS

Acknowledgements are due to the following, where some of these poems first appeared:

boomerang.com: 'from *The Arcades Project*'
Poetry London: 'Blessing', 'The Myth of Flight', 'After an Accident'
Stand: 'Oven Gloves' and 'The Muse's Lament'
Verse: 'Glaucus to Endymion'

'The Gas Poker' won a prize in the 2004 Bridport Prize poetry competition.

CONTENTS

Orphan Sites

AIRPORTS

The smallest have the quality of sky,
that nimbus which we know them by,
their Nissen huts pretending to be grass,
runways like hands held palm-up
to coax down aircraft out of ether's grip,
the wind-sock's orange gravitas,
and out beyond the verge of bush and ditch
the prayer-wheel of the radar dish.

The open windows of the terminus
catch the light and bend the air,
making this piece of earth a telescope
to bring the improbably distant close,
for those lost souls who stand behind the wire
and blindly scan the clouds for hope.

SUPERSTITION

for Hilary

The owls are shifting in the oaks,
nocturnal wings dreaming of black velvet.
In the late afternoon business of other birds
they stir themselves.

To them I will attribute nothing
as I sit among the waist-high grasses
which reach above my table top, their heads
ready to disintegrate,

although I *am* haunted (as are most,
I've found). With the threat of Nemesis.
With an unspoken fear that what I fear may come.
With terrible rumours.

How far is the range of their hunting?
Their first cough or wheeze at twilight does not
claim lives, but other ideas I hear and which are harder
to countenance

I accept without question. I can hear
the strimmer's feathery whisk coming nearer
across the field and marvel that no hide-out is safe.
The satellites

have this field in their frame, its birch
and willow crowns mapped out as they mature
and spread. Soon my rectangular, white plastic table
will come into view.

No need for owls. The dark edges
we cannot see within ourselves are starting
to assume their shapes, to unfurl their velvet wings,
starting to stir themselves.

BYRON'S GONDOLIER

We wait all afternoon for them
but still they hang about the quay
for ages, taking in the sunset,
the rarer air God help me,

and then his majesty commands
me turn about and row back up
the lagoon so he can show his pal
a better station. There we stop

and as the rafters of the sky
smoulder he likens that hoarse bell
to a soul which, locked inside the skull,
keens like a madman in his cell –

in mourning for a better world.
Sweet Jesus. Then there's more debate
on matters so high-flown all fall
to Earth for lack of lift. It's late

for fuck's sake. Now can we go home?
No. They want to loll here for hours.
It doesn't seem to bother them
that night has fallen and the powers

of nature brew themselves a storm.
Like two lost boats without their anchors
these two bump their gunwales, yaw
and wallow. What a pair of wankers.

BOY

Back Forest was the place we had stick fights in –
my brother and me pitted against my father;
the thrill of dancing out the way, the lazy flight
of branches through the forest's smoky light,
the joy at landing direct hits, the rush to gather
stockpiles, arsenals, an impregnable position

upslope from the enemy – and once as a young man
I fell in love and hunted down her gasped surprise
through its brakes and coverts, over unkempt launds
and fallen oaks to wrestle with her on the autumn ground,
tumbling down in Catherine wheels of leaves, her eyes,
up close to mine, full of its broken shafts of sun.

COLD SPELL

Back from the grave my mother chills the air
as she used to. "It wasn't like that at all," she says,
speaking from a frosted pane on the stairs.

She shakes herself into her shape – quite
a feat after nineteen years under ground:
"You know I did my best for you, despite

the sacrifices – which I gladly made,"
almost as if now dead she spoke her mind,
who in this life left much she meant unsaid.

My childhood passed as if she wasn't there.
What I remember most was her blank face
turned to the window, empty as the air.

There are many things I am tempted to say
like: "Yes, but you always lied" or "You never asked
what I thought and wouldn't listen anyway",

but I half believe the claim because I know
how tenderly I felt at first for her flesh
that winter underneath its ice tattoo.

But now it is the season of stone-hard ground
and she is back again in modern dress,
a new lilt to her voice, more refined.

"Give me what I never had," I say, and love's
blast furnace barbecues my face. It's still
not what I want but I can't get enough

and slam out to the cold night, leaving you
your angry tears, to gulp the icy air
and breathe the distance as I used to do.

AT GUN

Gun is the place where three roads met
for centuries, a Pennine hill
without a profile, its arched back
covered with burnt heather and white
quartz fists, the place we went for picnics
when I was young, its spirit still

with a kind of exhaustion, a fallow place
and full of sombre indecision.
I am thinking about the boy I was,
of those lonely weekend afternoons,
the sound of wind soughing in thorn,
as I walk through cuckoo-spit and pines

in the long plantation where its walls
are broken now and on the bent spine
of the ridge where the gibbet once stood
to guard the roads, an unfenced bull
brings back that old fear of mine,
that I would always be afraid.

THE END OF TYRANNY

A good third of the class
looked forward to it,
but did not know where to start.
We were just learning the ropes

and would have been surprised to learn
it happened on holiday
when my brother and I threw
our father onto the sofa.

COMPASS

A strip of pasture backing on the house
dipped to a brook, an ordinary field
which for thirteen years was the universe:
this above all impressed the child.

Unnamed. A few cows maybe by the hedge.
But in his thirst to name he called each clump
of common bent, canary grass or sedge
its own: Hag-Hog; the Bollin Broad; Mad Tump.

Of course I can still smell the pollen haze
or feel the dew drench through my baseball boots,
the vast prairie that was the holidays
stretching as far as lunch, explore the roots

of elms along the field's far borders, count
the countless magpies in the trees of dawn,
when the immediate was paramount:
a gold-leaf glitter off immortal corn,

the technicolour hoverflies and bees,
their zig-zags patterning a warm air pearled
with marbled sticky liquid from the trees,
each scent a door which opened a new world.

Sitting here now below the thundering skies,
fragile is how it was: the thin brick walls
so chancy, the field now built upon, and memories –
weak impulses between the dying cells.

THE PENNINES

From my parents' bedroom there they were
like mist, a faint raised edge of deeper greys
along the whole horizon; on clear days
so detailed they stood shimmeringly near

and seemed to float upon the air. I looked
to them for hearsay of the world beyond
the desk or face that swam in my foreground,
some myth or stone my lonely soul had worked,

some map-traced journey to augmented lands
where valleys hide their heads in scarves of mist
and brown moors break out into limestone karst.
Such boundaries are a playpen for the mind,

containing it and helping it to grow.
I ride the updraft over Wildboarclough,
a balsa glider built to soar above
whatever obstacle outcrops below.

IN HIS ELEMENT

Let rain fall on me
rain in all its guises:
slanting spears of rain
falling across Caledonian pines;

rain which almost doesn't fall
but forms on your eyelashes
or drips from the soused birch,
mizzle, Scotch mist, smirr;

cupped handfuls of rain
the cheeky wind chucks in your face
as you toil up an incline
beside an angry loch;

the kind of rain which fills
forests with the scent of resin;
rain the eraser wiping out
whole valleys of black tenements;

rain as the sudden storm
which leaves its trailing wraiths
and runs like foam off crags,
filling the empty glens with roars;

whole river-reddening days
of rain in its forms of ecstasy –
thunderplumps, cloudbursts, cataracts –
let all of them in one day fall on me.

DAVID CARGILL

For years I was only known as Julian
Turner, too ashamed of them; as spies
they lived the lives of sleepers, buried deep.

But now my middle names are out again.
They have their own friends I don't recognise;
hold their counsel which they closely keep

and hatch their plots, their treachery revealed
through covert operations: they want to go
north of the border. It's where they're from.

And so the Act of Union is repealed,
their own right to a legislature grows.
They have begun moves for a referendum.

BY THE IAPETUS OCEAN

In my mind's hand I hold the sea
that shrinks upon the back of three
illimitable rafts of rock,
or witness mountains build from shock-

after-shock as their collisions close
the once-wide ocean: lava floes,
each earthquake buckling through the crust
which hardens, cools, cracks at the thrust

of magma rising. Volcano arcs
stud the horizon, raining sparks
and bomb-rock, pumice rafts and smoke
making it look like Ragnarok;

pillow lavas couch the earth
and cast the country of my birth.
I sit still as exhausted waves
fall on the sand where nothing moves,

so many beaches they will lie
thousands of metres deep on Skye,
each one without footprint or fossil;
shadowy, silent and colossal

peaks rising above me, their siltstone
and greywacke buttressing England's bones.
So much for the bigger picture.
At the sea's edge I trace the suture

where nations join and run my hand
along the fault-lines of our land,
touch where the Atlantic will begin,
tell how the ancient forest's pines

will grow from the rocks' soil, its wash
of loch-side oaks and mountain ash.
I watch its Alp-height wear away
down to the shape it has today.

MORAG

You came highly recommended on the teen grapevine
from the impossible distance of 10 miles away:
Wallingford Grammar School. Your words ran
ahead, a raft of feverish odes, risqué

laments for burning concubines. We met
once on the bridge. You walked me to the graveyard,
dragged me into the lodge to meet a prat
who made plaster casts of penises that stood

like toadstools on their chipboard base. You asked
me to interpret them. I must have been
a disappointment, tongue-tied, too aghast
to even try for cool. I have forgotten

most of what I knew of you – surname,
face – but not that sprawling stream of words
tumbling upon themselves which seemed to come
unmediated from their source. I heard

some fourth-hand gossip gilding you with horse,
hooch and stalking Bowie; left alone
in a corridor when you couldn't stay the course.
Was that true? And did your spirit drown

in welcome silence? Was that a joy to learn?
I doubt it. You would find me much the same:
still awkwardness itself; afraid to yearn;
unconscious of how cold I sometimes seem.

Listen. Words were a gift to me. A prayer
for comfort in the emptiness inside,
a way to move the world without being there,
an echo. Is it worth it? You decide.

PARTNER

To travel through landscapes like those imagined moons
of childhood, white rock, forever white rock, limestone
or quartz, whether bangling dales with their white walls
or breaking up below frost into cross-hatchings, chards,
brittle fingers veined with iron and feldspar as it is here,
always to travel through places such as this, to visit her
I go alone.

Rain-water steeping me, shimmering off brilliant sheets,
berating in a thousand voices from the burns, churning
in the sheiling stream, a chorus of sedge-soak overflows,
mist-washing beside the path the 10p-sized matt beetles
like plastic, the alpine gentian and black moss of screes,
the lunar wilderness of ash-white rock, where, between
the peat-hag lilies

and the tree-line out of sight below, a rowan has put root
into the crystal fragments at my feet, its one-inch trunk
divided just above the ground beside a sandstone boulder,
its two-fold nature beautifully at one, inclining to Slioch
which stands above the mirror of itself in ink loch water,
witched with its own grace, companionable beside me,
shoulder to shoulder.

OVEN GLOVES

They're not new: turned from soft to stiff
by the countless batters, pizzas, bakes
I've soiled, stained and burned them with,
they hold their own chronology
of our domestic life. I take
this cake I'm minding out and place
their grizzly hands around my face
to feel our years embracing me.

AT WALCOTT

The full moon marooned between
the horns of chimney pots,
the stars fat and sugary;
the Insurance Company massive
and back-lit, its arms crossed –

something about the light tonight
brings back that Norfolk shore,
its cascading zither of stars,
their electromagnetic pulses
crawling across our scalps,

both of us taken by a fever
of wishing to approach
until we almost merged,
so close we seemed to share
the same mind

as the moon silvered the frontal lobes
of thunderheads above the sea,
rising as dirigibles of bliss
over the horizon to hang
an illustration in front of us,

to magnify each glance, each touch,
each prefatory kiss. That night
we began construction on the first
foundations, pouring the Ready-Mix
for our own footings,

to support the clouds and their high lancets.
It's been a good year for skies –
like tonight's thrown-back storm hoods
exposing the moon's mother-of-pearl;
and dark winged rafts

break off and drift apart.

OUT OF MY KNOWLEDGE

John Clare on Emmonsales Heath

The furze chased gold leaf to the sun,
the grass blades bent their backs
to catch the silky sprigs of light
that sprouted by the track.

A place where I could be myself;
a white moth fluttered by
and crickets whispered foreign tongues
to cabbage butterflies.

With woken spirits I walked on
in circles round the world
which seemed transformed from ordinary
to alchemists' new gold.

The birds' nests in the bracken wept,
the wind stirred pools of milk,
the long day seemed a morning long
and silver spider silk.

I have a mind for field and whin,
to the world's end I go
to look down from the edge of it
and scry the deeps below.

Will I return? And will the lanes
be recognisable?
Will Langley Bush still seem the same
and ditches be as full?

No, there will be a difference
to Glinton's needle spire,
all roads will bend round to myself
and larks rise higher, higher.

THE MYTH OF FLIGHT

Straight through the fence my body-weight
propelling me, timber and tinder,
I squat on a parked car's roof as springs
explode inside my musculature
and help me hover in the air.
My mind is slipping out of gear.

I can sense gravel against my cheek,
in my hair, the throb of friction-burns
fresh on my skin, which comfort me.
My body fears my thoughts, my brain
is full of lorries hollering,
their wheels, the kerb I'm lying on.

I flew. I always knew I could.
I wait, grit in my mouth, and feel
the cost of living and a sudden
urge to ground the airborne soul,
to feel the floor. I wedge myself
between the car wheels and the wall.

AFTER AN ACCIDENT

it comes back in bits – the sudden bend
a flash of wall too close – tarmac then
nothing   a huge percussion to the ribs
pain as their spring bounces you back
to where you lie spinning in the road
the neon sky settling above you
like a blanket – headlights wagging
their fingers – your breath in sobs
which stab your lungs   a nagging stillness
asking you for sleep
                            you wink in again
figures bent over you now
low words lost in the background hiss
as if you were a local beauty spot
where people choose to stop at night
and gasp – sounds are taking their time
to reach you
                        as if a sudden resolution
of slowness had been passed   you
could lie here forever
the camber arching under your back
a ticking in your ears
your mind   counting down
the precious seconds

STOCKTAKING

Trunk

Small pools of phlegm form overnight
in my lungs, harmless as dew. I moan
and there appear six pearls of light
on plastic, see-through sheets of bone.

Leg

A moon of black that fits the knee,
a hole in the foot which pierces half-
way to the sole, a purulent scree
of lacerations down the calf:
a lava lamp of bruising goes
down from the thigh to cloud the toes.

Dreams

I sleep a lot as if my brain
had artificial worlds to make:
a string of peaks, paths bright with rain
and sudden drops to help me wake.

Pain

They help you through it. On my wrist
a pump of morphine sits. Cool gel
fattens my veins. I must exist
but how and where I cannot tell.

THE MUSE'S LAMENT

Poor fumbler. I am reduced
to doing manly things
badly; all fingers and thumbs.
But look, look at my rings –

so delectable and bright
inside the gloves of his hands
like stars in the bruised grease
of his fist; no wedding bands

ever shone so. Intimacy
is frowned on. He doesn't know
me well, even in the mirror
where I almost show

as pearls in his penumbra.
I lend him deftness of touch
for his love affairs; he does not
appreciate it much.

I am cramped, bent out of shape
by gravity's greater power
and skulk about inside
him like a slut or cower

in a corner of his mind
to whisper "death is sweet"
into our inner silence
where two of us compete.

For I could spread behind
his head, a hint of perfume
when he hangs his coat
or walks across the room;

my weightless tears could burst
that dam of his, could grace
his gaucheness, wipe the worry
off his empty face,

but all he does is curse
my weakness, cut his arms
to shut me up and steel
himself against my charms.

Returning home alone
in the car at night he'll feel
my strength, a subtle nudge
which knocks the steering wheel.

MIDLIFE

A blonde girl in our library downstairs,
in one of those easy chairs that sink too deep,
the wall-lamps glinting off her hennaed hair,
her bright and clever eyes closed as in sleep.

I can remember how that smile of hers
would run at me and burrow in my chest,
how curious the sense of fit, how cold
my hand against her buttock or her breast.

It's not just this, but if I'm honest too,
her nervous hands, bewitching jealousies
and jump-cut moods provided an excuse
to live exalted in diminished days.

Anyone guess how I killed her? Will I forget
her quickly? Is there something to regret?

GLAUCUS TO ENDYMION

Best of all she liked my huge fish thigh
flapping between her legs.
This excited her she said
although I must confess I couldn't tell:
there used to be a veil she drew
across the space between us –
to starve herself to greater pleasure
so she claimed, fondling my hairs and scales.

But when I watched her, driven by desire
to find her out, among her herds,
gently tendering them
the titbits from her hands, a look
would wrap her and her lids tremble, like this.
Afterwards I nibbled at the crumbs their lips
had missed and felt vast ribs of oxen
circle me, thickening in my chest,
halter and bridle
growing in my skull as bars of bone
and leather leashes tying me to her.

This was how she made her beasts: from men.
I felt their every bruise, as if bent out of shape,
my body and my terror boxed
in some small cupboard, crushed up close
in cramp, my knees pressed to my lungs
leaving bruises there.

I did escape,
but now I wish myself back in her pastures
wild with those spirit skeins she unleashed
from her hands: the way they split and flew.
Age is a worse vice than her cattle drugs;
it bends me back on myself
in bonds of flesh which cannot be removed.
Circe raided flesh to cheat it. Now
her curse of years begins to draw
me back to her. I wind up outside her house,
eager to learn.

REPULSION

I

The mind shies away from it – a reflex·
like the way two pieces of magnetic chess
pressed base-to-base flip round and stand apart.
Anathema, it stops you in your tracks

as you labour on the details of your will,
pausing over interment or cremation –
the cold constriction of eternity
boxed up beneath four hundredweight of soil,

your skin blisters, your organs liquefy,
a purge of putrefying froth leaks from
all orifices, every feature lost
as your face swells to bursting and your eyes

spring out, your brain begins to drizzle down
your cheeks, your sternum ruptures from the force
of methane and ammonia, swollen
like some absurd and slush-filled flesh balloon,

or else, on rollers as the curtains shut
and just before the piped hymn whines its bars
of *I will fear no evil*, the gas jets roar
at 1,700 degrees Fahrenheit

and you put on a light show for yourself
as your salts go up and the flesh is melted off,
your bones, your bones are burned from white to black
and back to white again, their powder proof

of your fragility as lastly all
affinity between your parts breaks down
and you are sieved as ash – a pause so long
both options pass before your sorry soul.

II

Rather, strap me out above the moors
in a sky burial, my eyes eaten by jackdaws,
the great rock of the Chevin at my back
ticking, as my world's goods are unpacked.

REMINISCO

for Chris Lawson

They come up the steps of the Palace Hotel, Buxton,
twilight soft as satin and *that* look
they had when they were taken has not gone
but is transformed to something stranger, like

their gait or characters which are now worn
as more external, like the pom-pom blossoms
of cherry on the lawn, raised to the moon.
Through some anomaly I feel at home,

and almost think that all the loved dead might
drift up to me through this embalming dark.
I often dreamed such things and yet the light
which plays upon their features has the quirk

of memory as if two eras overlapped
and childhood laid itself on yesterday.
They are dressed to dance and take the steps
with all their unlived longing still in place,

their full zest for life without fear or fret.
Their languid movements perfectly express
frustration at the timing of their death
but are more blithe for being bodiless,

although their flesh is solid like my own
but free of the slow steep in the stain of woe,
their doubts about themselves quite forgotten:
I watch them move as they were meant to do

and join them on the vast and starry floor,
my mood a perfect mix of joy and calm.
I start to dance the *Punk Rock Troubadour*.
They give me gooseflesh. Brush against my arm.

THE EDGE

I know of some who struggle to survive
beyond the furthest circle of the sun,
whose days are drawn in, narrow, north enough
for no light to leach under their horizon;

whose daybreaks are a promise never kept,
their hopes Novaya Zemlya effects –
hallucinated suns the ice reflects
from other latitudes – who intercept

these images, a lifeline they are thrown,
who use illusion as a photophore
to help them live in darkness and alone.

It is not understood how they endure;
their infinite resourcefulness unknown.
We say they suffer from a calenture.

THE PAUPER LUNATIC ASYLUM, MENSTON

Outside the village life is usual –
we run our errands late by car
or shop alone among abstracted malls,
our faces which are empty of desire

our bodies which belong to someone else
automatons that dance to different tunes;
and other times below the clock-tower bells
inside the village with its fetching lawns

and sighing trees we learn to sing again,
our voices purified by long displays
of joy and fear, our faces window panes
where if you look you see our yesterdays –

how they blossom with aplomb, our ersatz
visitors who talk to mobile phones
and we who cry, cry loudly in our hats.
All that we do we learn to do alone.

Some spirit left the world a while ago
unannounced and unseen, departing like
an angel on sad wings. It turned once slow-
ly in the sky and left this longing ache.

from THE ARCADES PROJECT

I turn the corner and in Global Video
one mouth comes down on another.
As the lips meet, the silhouettes are marmite
against its yellow lid. How hard it is
to see colours, how hard to be alone.

Comme il faut: the chain of paving flags
sleek with the rain is drawing me forwards
always through the subway of the crowd,
a wind-tunnel of souls which drift and tumble
over one another towards a destination

unseen in the splashes of conversation
which half drown me, make me splutter and spit,
following my own labyrinth which winds up
out of my mind with its deadly secret into this
world on which the wind prints my delible outline

against the shifting wash of neighbourhoods,
as if I strolled in the mountains, those dead
tableaux vivants, the image of my lovers
taking the air, inspired, flicking between one
then another, interchangeable, each

demanding their own particular apple,
a kind of vortex in which, submersible,
I douse all traces of myself in a skin
so varnished by inattention that I slip
through unnoticed, giving nothing back,

unreadable, a lozenge the tongue can't erode,
and believe me I *am* tongued, elbowed, pressed
by those whose faces I can read, this mass
of particles in Brownian motion in which a man
may search on every other face in vain

for a sign which marks that person out and when
he finds one marked so by an urgent frown,
remote half-smile or aura and confronts him,
like as not he will be staring at himself
in a lit shop-window, his eyes ablaze

with borrowed candles and a thousand glints
off the shop goods' rich delights, as though in seeking
another he had only wished to find himself
between hoardings, shuffling and stumbling
below their enormous gestures, their kaleidoscope

of colours, their arbitrary enamouredness,
trying to take it all in and remain impartial,
always walking, the last man left alive,
as if the noun consumer were the last attempt
to halt, for a second, the certainty of being eaten.

I will sit down beside the river of the gutter
and weep; beside the gargantuan drain I'll keep
vigil, a witness to the loneliness inside
which seems to fill the Universe, the fear
of someone's mouth descending on my own.

THE GAS POKER

Already tiger stripes and blue-
black ribs of curling gloss, it chokes
this field of ours its jaws fixed to
the highest log, its long tongue smokes,

and coughs its arcs of embers out.
How easy was that? Only a few
fire-lighter bricks tucked under it
and we could feel the night withdraw:

the modern versions of those totems
which made our fifties' fires bright
and in un-centrally-heated homes
glowed red-hot in the anthracite –

the gas pokers I still feel warm
towards for warding off the cold,
as predecessors coaxed a flame
from coal with newspapers they held

or whirled a stick to strike a spark
in tinder, warmth which won't snuff out:
an implement which left no mark
except its faithful dragon snout

snorting in minds like mine. It's strange
and almost our own signature
how we accept that all things change,
forgetful what has gone before,

but if it's in dispute how we
remember this old caulked-with-soot-
and-clinker rod, let it not be
like its only entry on the net

in *The Dictionary of Human Cruelty*;
may it instead be as comforter,
a bringer of heat, poor man's jewellery,
companion to those who shiver

lonely beside an empty hearth,
their fleece, their winter samovar,
their word of welcome to this Earth
as these cheap fire-lighters are.

THE CRADLE SONG OF
THE GRANDMOTHERS

You feel me in your hair at night,
a clasp and surge of pain,
and perturbations by your ear
which sound inside your brain.

I claw your eyelids open, peer
into those pools of light,
beating my wings against the cool
smooth surface of your fright.

I shadow you in daytime too,
an echo in your mind
which bleeds the colour from the sky
and keeps you from your kind.

Under my ancient gaze your dreams
dissolve in sonar clicks;
I empty every pore of you
and fill you with my tricks.

I move in your unconsciousness
like dark wind on a shore;
where twice your height the breakers crash
down with a hollow roar.

The black groynes stand against the sand
and tremble on its glow;
their fingers jab the ebbing tide,
the sand drifts pale as snow.

The empty beach goes on and on
beside the massing sea;
your shadow flits inside your head
and looks back guiltily.

My death has made no difference,
I know more than you know;
the dead may go on living where
the living dare not go.

KINTARO GROWS OLD

*Kintaro, in Japanese folklore, was a feral child who went on
to free Edo (modern Tokyo) from a terrorising band of thugs.
He is celebrated during Kodomo-no-hi, or Children's Day.*

When young I scarcely knew my size or strength,
a cub of bears who couldn't have their own:
their shaggy natures lent me mammal-sense,
the tang of fear and how to stand alone,
to match brute force with wit, muscle for muscle
in the dense busks and stubbings, taught me how deep
all habits run, the parts still animal
which have their honour and define our scope.

My gift was chasing on the heels of fright.
The truth is, I doubted I was strong.
I thought my body frail, my build slight.
Much later when I had to face the gang,
take in their looks and sniff their reek of fear,
I was surprised at such a simple thing –
that bullying or going off to war
would stop if terror could sit still and sing.

There comes a time all giants learn their size.
It takes ages for this knowledge to evolve,
as if the body was a crude disguise
which slows the truth or makes it hard to prove.
Some find it in the fear in people's faces,
others in comments lovers make at night
confessing comfort in our curl-up places.
I found out mine when age began to bite.

I know that I may not refuse my fate:
the symbol of a courage scarcely felt
to frighten children, urge them on to fight,
a woodland hulk which bears and combat built,
a smiling oaf to keep the thieves from meat,
a Mr Sturdy Oak. I'm none of these,
just one small son his parents couldn't beat.
May God prevent the strengthening of boys.

SECOND WIND

I

The wild west wind shakes autumn's gaudy rags
to bits, a poltergeist which thrashing frees
the skeins of leaves to flail among the crags;

fragments of tile, snap-offs from flattened trees
and wounded crows skitter across the roads;
the fervid sky, the fevers of disease

strain in the air above the jack-knifed loads,
the flattened caravans and crawling wires
of fallen power lines lost in the clouds,

as if a blight had blown in with the bonfires,
the puddles rainbowing like turpentine,
the splayed-out road kill and exploded tyres;

the pegged-out black gloves glisten, shake and sign
a maddened language of the peregrine.

II

Listen to it work – a vast, exhaling howl
which rolls up in a ball of air all seeds,
all germs and shakes each consonant and vowel

out of their senses, scatters them in screeds
as language rearranged and cast as curse.
The eggs of all things blow among the reeds,

infected, left to drift, the universe
a map of cyclones trapped in isobars
wailing and worsening, its larynx hoarse.

I knew this wind before I knew its scars,
its mind-wash, its horse-maddening routine,
its close-knit rage of dust; I saw its powers

instinct and moving in a world between
the actual and the ghost in the machine.

III

That which awoke our island fastnesses
(I know you cannot hear) with blades of waves
which slice the long-shore drift, to listlessness

and people dreaming their foreshortened lives
in tired foliage of autumnal thought,
bring damage and destruction. On the graves

of Little England dance your wild cavort,
your reservoirs of methane stored as kinds
of crystal on the ocean bed abort

and bleed into the air, bring to an end
our stale routine, the airways where I ran;
in blind contumely, torture and distend

the wilful artifice of Caliban
upon the rack of iron made by man.

IV

Out here the birches bend in the great wind,
their pennies sashay down the aisles of gold
to a new music – emptiness of mind

which bids farewell to what it cannot hold,
and breathes in with your breath – and ribs of light
are falling in arcs across the lonely road.

Shine if you can inside the gale's throat,
a small spark swallowed by the air's abyss,
a guttering before you are snuffed out.

You will not be particularly missed.
The world renews itself and grows again
from its own root; all creatures which exist

shall be swept up before this hurricane
and washed like seeds across a clean terrain.

HOLMROOK

Cumberland, 1957

According to family myth, this place-name was
my first word. I have (is this the truth?)
a memory of both parents turning round
to me in the back seat of the Ford Pop –
the only time that I engaged them both?

There must have been a backdrop to that drive –
some rain-washed Lakeland farm, a plethora
of cattle grids, a picnic by a C-road
on the moors, where wool writhed on barbed wire –
but everything of that has been re-mastered.

We were at a guest house on the coast at Grange.
The breakfast window overlooked the sea
so unpredictably: sometimes the world
was blue and others just an endless gold.
I was surprised at such variety.

I do remember there were no Cornflakes
unlike at home. I have no memory
at all of what I have been told I saw,
the river white with whorls of deadly milk.
How much could I pick up from adult talk?

How was it strange, the look I got that day?
I still love that name for itself, its sound
a resonance and residence of birds –
and for a first hint how my mum would die,
as if there were an added power to words.

IN THE IRONHASH HILLS

Dumfries, 1986

The World Cup was on, so it was June
above the Solway Firth – a vast palm of light
where you could read the lifelines of the tides
etched into blazing sand. Here for two weeks
I walked at random in the hills and drank
my fill from crystal spate in cupped hands,
my body thirsting for its lucid mystery,
its rare, transforming touch. Another own goal.

THE SIGNALMAN

If Candace Pert is right that our chemistry
builds molecules which fuel emotion's train
and transports information to the brain
from the body's broad Republic, shouldn't we
through some small change be able to discern
exactly when a rogue cell starts dividing
relentlessly and throw a switch to turn
it safely down a harmless stretch of siding?

FOOTPRINTS

Some quality has drained from nature's dream
although its rare, cold grace still touches you,
perhaps inflected with a darker theme.

The spheres of rain that are not what they seem
are whole worlds on the leaves of feverfew –
some quality has drained from nature's dream.

While greens of spring and catkin tails redeem
the winter on the willows they renew,
they are affected by a darker theme.

The morning mist dispersing in a steam
of horsetail wraiths is not the mist you knew –
some quality has drained from nature's dream

and evening clouds' empurpled curdled cream
of strange and out-of-kilter pink and blue
have been infected by a darker theme:

the summer storms are urgent and extreme.
And though all this seems beautiful and true,
some quality has drained from nature's dream.
It is directed by a darker theme.

ORPHAN SITES

At first light this one shimmers in a veil
of corrugated air, its apron spread
with dust and rubble where the ghost of oil
fades from the forecourt; silhouetted sheds,
abandoned drums, old tyres in dim relief
against the shoulder of the city's rim
reflected in the puddles left by brief
before-dawn bursts of rain, their rainbow skim
like breakdown products of old promises;
all quarantined by wire mesh from the sprawl
of suburbs which would once have fed off this,
a mocking echo of the water hole.

If you have walked this way among the parts
of Earth no one will own an interest in,
where logos vanish from the public charts
and tanks begin their rusted weepings in
the water-table where the toxins flow;
or strolled among the jetsam from a vast
and cumbersome machine, then you will know
our sense of unbelonging is the cost
of all our man-made wildernesses and
why unadopted places seem so fit,
as if a soul instinctively will find
a landscape which it knows resembles it.

WINDOW

in memory of Michael Donaghy

He has taken off to influence
the weather, knowing where
the angels are and how to work
their weird mechanicals,

his flickering identities –
a thousand strips of window –
raining down in radio silence
from the winter heavens.